CW01091062

50 Quick Ways to

Motivate and Engage Your Students

By Mike Gershon

Starting your professional learning journey with Academies Enterprise Trust

www.academiesenterprisetrust.org

#teachAET

About the Author

Mike Gershon is a teacher, trainer and writer. He is
the author of twenty books on teaching, learning and
education, including a number of bestsellers, as well
as the co-author of one other. Mike's online
resources have been viewed and downloaded more
than 2.5 million times by teachers in over 180
countries and territories. He is a regular contributor
to the Times Educational Supplement and has
created a series of electronic CPD guides for TES
PRO. Find out more, get in touch and download free
resources at www.mikegershon.com

Training and Consultancy

Mike is an expert trainer whose sessions have received acclaim from teachers across England. Recent bookings include:

- *Improving Literacy Levels in Every Classroom*, St Leonard's Academy, Sussex

- *Growth Mindsets, Effective Marking and Feedback* Ash Manor School, Aldershot

- *Effective Differentiation,* Tri-Borough Alternative Provision (TBAP), London

Mike also works as a consultant, advising on teaching and learning and creating bespoke materials for schools. Recent work includes:

- *Developing and Facilitating Independent Learning,* Chipping Norton School, Oxfordshire

- *Differentiation In-Service Training,* Charles Darwin School, Kent

If you would like speak to Mike about the services he can offer your school, please get in touch by email: mike@mikegershon.com

Other Works from the Same Authors

Available to buy now on Amazon:

How to use Differentiation in the Classroom: The Complete Guide

How to use Assessment for Learning in the Classroom: The Complete Guide

How to use Questioning in the Classroom: The Complete Guide

How to use Discussion in the Classroom: The Complete Guide

How to Teach EAL Students in the Classroom: The Complete Guide

More Secondary Starters and Plenaries

Secondary Starters and Plenaries: History

Teach Now! History: Becoming a Great History Teacher

The Growth Mindset Pocketbook (with Professor Barry Hymer)

How to be Outstanding in the Classroom

Also available to buy now on Amazon, the entire 'Quick 50' Series:

50 Quick and Brilliant Teaching Ideas

50 Quick and Brilliant Teaching Techniques

50 Quick and Easy Lesson Activities

50 Quick Ways to Help Your Students Secure A and B Grades at GCSE

50 Quick Ways to Help Your Students Think, Learn, and Use Their Brains Brilliantly

50 Quick Ways to Motivate and Engage Your Students

50 Quick Ways to Outstanding Teaching

50 Quick Ways to Perfect Behaviour Management

50 Quick and Brilliant Teaching Games

50 Quick and Easy Ways to Outstanding Group Work

50 Quick and Easy Ways to Prepare for Ofsted

50 Quick and Easy Ways Leaders can Prepare for Ofsted

About the Series

The 'Quick 50' series was born out of a desire to provide teachers with practical, tried and tested ideas, activities, strategies and techniques which would help them to teach brilliant lessons, raise achievement and engage and inspire their students.

Every title in the series distils great teaching wisdom into fifty bite-sized chunks. These are easy to digest and easy to apply – perfect for the busy teacher who wants to develop their practice and support their students.

Acknowledgements

As ever I must thank all the fantastic colleagues and students I have worked with over the years, first while training at the Institute of Education, Central Foundation Girls' School and Nower Hill High School and subsequently while working at Pimlico Academy and King Edward VI School in Bury St Edmunds.

Thanks also to Alison and Andrew Metcalfe for a great place to write and finally to Gordon at KallKwik for help with the covers.

Table of Contents

Checklists

Time Limits

Humour

Prizes

Team Games

Meet and Greet

Thank You

Karaoke

Riddles

Optical Illusions

Movement

Journey into Space

The Wonders of the World

Pictionary

Taboo

Charades

Just a Minute

Props

Take on the Role of a Character

Give them Independence

Let Students Take Decisions

Relevant Connections

Useful Feedback

Introduction

Welcome to '50 Ways to Motivate and Engage Your Students.'

We all know how important motivation and engagement are in the classroom. Great lessons get students on board, get them interested and, as a result, get them learning.

But how do we make sure pupils are always motivated and engaged?

This book sets out to answer that question by providing fifty different strategies, activities and techniques you can pick up and put into practice straight away.

The emphasis is practical throughout – all the ideas stem from my own experience as a teacher and trainer. They can all be applied across the curriculum and you can use them with different age groups as well.

One final thing. None of the entries are set in stone. You can adapt and alter any of them to fit your teaching style and the particular needs of your students, if you so wish.

Well, that leaves me with nothing more to say other than that I hope you enjoy the book and I hope the ideas inside help send those motivation and engagement levels soaring through the roof of your classroom!

Smile!

01 Smile and the world smiles with you.

Smile in the classroom and your students will start smiling as well.

It's human nature to respond positively to a smile. Of course, some teenagers may keep up a glum façade; after all, many see it as part of their job! But you don't need to let this stop you. Keep on smiling and the motivation levels of your class will soon start to spiral upwards.

Laugh!

02 Because laughter is infectious and it makes us feel good. If an opportunity arises to tell a joke or inject a bit of humour, grab hold of it. Share a chuckle with your students and watch how the atmosphere instantly lifts.

You can also use laughter to neutralise tricky situations or downplay the significance of off-task behaviour (in order to draw pupils' attention away from it and back towards the work).

It is useful to begin and end your lessons with a bit of laughter. This will create engagement and motivation at the start and see students leaving your classroom with a positive memory (increasing the likelihood that when they return next lesson they will recall positive connotations).

Set Firm and Clear Boundaries

03 This is important for a number of reasons.

First, we all like to know where we stand and what is expected of us, particularly in a learning situation. Firm and clear boundaries communicate this information simply and effectively.

Second, if you need to enforce the rules, this will be much easier if you can refer to the firm and clear boundaries you consistently outline and adhere to.

Third, the purpose of boundaries and rules in the classroom is to regulate behaviour and to create an understanding of how things are to pan out. Ensuring yours are firm and clear means life will be simpler and easier for your students. In turn, this will lead to higher levels of motivation and engagement.

Enforce the Rules

04 If you don't enforce the rules then negative things will happen: students will grow uncertain about what is acceptable and what is not acceptable; you will find it harder to get the behaviour you want; the fairness of punishments will be challenged; the general atmosphere in your classes will tend to deteriorate; you will not have the level of control necessary to ensure everyone makes great progress.

All of this will lead to a situation in which students become disengaged and struggle to maintain motivation.

Therefore, the best thing you can do is to consistently enforce your rules.

Model Great Manners

05 Politeness is a virtue. It engenders a sense of civility, respect and positivity (in the sense that good manners project a clear belief that one should think about others and treat them well). It is very hard – perhaps impossible – to be demotivated and disengaged by good manners.

Not only will your excellent etiquette help get pupils on board and feeling good about your lessons, but so too will it provide an exemplary model for them; one which they can copy so as to spread further motivation and engagement through the class as a whole.

Read Dale Carnegie

06 This one is an absolute must. Dale Carnegie's book, 'How to Win Friends and Influence People,' available on Amazon, can be re-read as a masterclass in how to motivate and engage students.

The reason is simple.

Much of the motivation and engagement in your classroom comes down to the relationships and rapport you develop with your students. And this is a function of your communication with them.

Communicate better, with greater skill, care and attention, and you are more likely to have a class who are motivated and engaged. Read Dale Carnegie and you'll find a whole host of practical ideas and techniques you can use to achieve this end.

Listen Genuinely

07 When you are listening to your pupils – whether they are talking to you about their work, what they did on the weekend or what they think about a particular idea – listen genuinely.

That is, pay attention to what they are saying (the form as well as the content of their words) before responding in a way which demonstrates you were genuinely listening.

This technique makes pupils feel appreciated and important. As such, it meets one of the core psychological needs all of us possess. Having these needs met and seeing the genuineness of your engagement will motivate pupils to work hard.

Reference Popular Culture (Badly)

08 Popular culture tends to form a large part of students' lives. They watch television, listen to music and access the internet for leisure. Keeping track of a little bit of the popular culture aimed at the youth of today(!) is a great way to facilitate engagement.

You can name-drop the popular culture you pick up on during your lessons or refer to it in relation to some part of the subject you are teaching. This will do two things. First, it will invoke a reference point which, for pupils, connects immediately to good memories and experiences. Second, it will indicate to students that you know a little bit about their world.

One of the best ways to reference popular culture is to do it (deliberately) badly. For example, by getting a name wrong or pronouncing something incorrectly. This is subtly self-deprecating. It will make pupils laugh and help to positively bind them into your lesson.

Ask Questions

09 This entry splits into two parts.

First, ask questions connected to the topic. Ask them to individual students, pairs, groups and the whole class. Ask them so that pupils have the opportunity to think about and discuss their opinions and ideas. Use open questions to facilitate this.

Second, ask questions unconnected to the topic, such as:

- How's your day going?

- What did you do over the weekend?

- What lessons do you have this afternoon?

When we ask questions we invite people to share with us. We invite them to let us into their minds. We indicate that we are interested in them and in their thoughts. This is engaging and, in a classroom context, motivational.

Remember Things (Especially Names)

10 If you ask your students questions about their lives, interests, hobbies and so on, remember the answers they share with you. Otherwise, you will give the impression that you are not really interested and only asked for reasons of show.

Even more important is remembering names.

The sooner you learn the names of all the students you teach, the sooner you will be able to communicate with them genuinely, build rapport and indicate the fact that you think they are important (because, if we don't know the name of someone we work with on a regular basis, what does that imply – whether true or not – about our opinion of them?).

Radiate Energy and Enthusiasm

11 Granted, this is not always easy.

On a grey and dank Monday morning, after you've spent half the weekend marking books, and you know that open evening is coming up on Thursday, the inclination to energy and enthusiasm can be difficult to find.

But find it you must! And if you can't find it, fake it. Pretend you are energetic and enthusiastic. Convey this idea to your students – they don't need to know the truth, after all.

In the classroom, it is up to you to set the tone. Never forget this. If you want motivation and engagement (as we all do!) radiate motivation and engagement yourself; pupils will follow and the mood will lift, whatever the starting point.

Vary the Pace

12 Slow things down. Speed them up. Make them manic. Calm them right down, almost to a standstill. Varying the pace makes things interesting. If you don't believe me, just think of a piece of music you love, a favourite film or a great book. It is highly likely that the pace in each one of these will vary.

You can vary the pace in your lessons by using different activities. Over time it is even possible to develop a sense of what a class requires (usually by observing movements, body language and conversations). Responding to this will allow you to maximise engagement and motivation by varying the pace of your lessons.

Rearrange the Classroom

13 A change is as good as a rest.

Every day students come into your classroom and see the same set up. There's nothing wrong with this of course, but a change can have seriously positive consequences. It mixes things up, creates a feeling of variety and excitement, and throws up new possibilities and potentials.

You might rearrange your classroom completely or just modify a little bit of it. You might decide to keep the changes or you might choose to make them a one-off alteration.

However you approach it, rearranging your classroom will most likely raise motivation levels and reignite your pupils' engagement with the lesson.

Get Out of the Classroom

14 While we're on the subject of the classroom, how about getting out of it? You could go into the corridor, onto the school field or you could do a walking tour of the school grounds (connected to the topic of study in some way).

Doing this will energise your pupils and give them a really memorable experience. Here are three examples of how you might get out of the classroom, just to get you started:

In Physics, test the resistance levels of different surfaces around the school.

In English, find different parts of the school to write poems about.

In Maths, calculate the dimensions of different school buildings.

Opportunities to Succeed

15 Experiencing success is a great motivator. It makes us believe in ourselves, gives us a sense of reward, and stimulates continued engagement with whatever it is we have succeeded in.

When planning your lessons, make sure you plan for students to succeed. This doesn't mean dumbing down or making things easy. Instead, it means planning so that pupils can engage with the work, experience challenge but, ultimately, be able to deal successfully with the problems and activities you place in front of them.

A good point to remember is that the experience of instant success is not actually that motivational in the long-run. Success needs to be earned if it is to have a significant impact on our psyches. Hence the importance of keeping your lessons challenging while also planning for success.

Good Old-Fashioned Praise

16 We all love to be praised. We like to know that we are doing a good job. We can spot false praise a mile off but may well remember genuine praise for half a lifetime.

Praise creates positive connotations, makes us feel valued and builds our self-esteem and confidence.

The best praise is specific, focussed on effort, grit and process (rather than end products) and given genuinely and with good grace.

Some students will regularly do things which draw praise. Others might not. In the latter case, look for opportunities; seek out things worth praising and then praise them.

Variety is the Spice of Life

17 This has been implicit in a number of the previous entries. It is worth considering in isolation however because of the importance of the fact (an importance which, perhaps, cannot be overstated).

Variety inspires us; it engages our minds; it livens up life, presenting us with novelty and new possibilities.

A canvas painted in a single colour is dull. One containing a range of hues and shades is not.

Vary the activities you use, the structure of your lessons and the way in which you teach. This will motivate and engage your students (and probably do the same for you as well).

One word of warning. Don't overdo the variety. We can all become jaded by excessive change. This is because for variety to be variety, we need a stable point of reference against which to compare it.

Plenaries on a Plate

18 Plenaries on a Plate is a fun and popular resource I have created and which you can download for free at www.mikegershon.com.

It is great for use at the end of lessons when you want to review or wrap-up the learning.

Students love the page of coloured dots (Slide 2) from which you can select plenaries (wrap-up or review activities) at random.

Try it out and see how it grabs the attention of your class.

The Starter Generator

19 The Starter Generator is a useful and popular resource I have created which you can download for free from my website.

It contains 120 starter activities which are appropriate for use across the age ranges and the curriculum. This means you can easily add variety to your lessons (see entry 17) by using it to help with your planning.

What is more, the activities contained within the Starter Generator are engaging, interesting, challenging and thought-provoking (and often all four!).

The Plenary Producer

20 The Plenary Producer is a useful and popular resource I have created which you can download for free from my website.

It contains 130 plenary (wrap-up or review) activities which are appropriate for use across the age ranges and the curriculum. This means you can easily add variety to your lessons (see entry 17) by using it to help with your planning.

What is more, the activities contained within the Plenary Producer will engage and motivate your students by helping them to reflect critically and creatively on the learning they have done during the course of your lesson.

Checklists

21 Checklists give students something to aim for. They make it very clear what will constitute success and what goals one needs to fulfil in order to be judged successful. Here are three examples of how you might use checklists in the classroom:

Provide checklists in the form of success criteria for activities and tasks.

Provide literacy checklists connected to spelling, punctuation and grammar.

Provide problem-solving checklists which pupils can refer to when they are stuck.

Having checklists on hand is motivational for three reasons. First, it helps students understand what is necessary for success. Second, it provides guidance for pupils to follow. Third, checklists can be referred to as and when, meaning that students feel like they have a safety net on hand, ready for use if they should need it.

Time Limits

22 Time limits turn standard tasks into beat-the-clock-races-against-time. This creates motivation, a sense of fun and a specific goal which all pupils in the class can aim for in the context of the lesson. In so doing it engages students, drawing them into what is essentially a game (beat the clock) where previously none existed.

Here are three ways you might like to use time limits:

- At the beginning of the lesson as part of a starter activity.

- Half-way through a lesson to up the pace.

- At the end of a lesson to motivate students who might be flagging.

Humour

23 We touched on humour in entry two where we looked at laughter's power to motivate and engage. Humour helps to create bonds, build rapport and lighten the mood. All these things engage and motivate. Here are three ways you might like to use humour in the classroom:

To self-deprecate. This sees you knowingly undermining the teacher-student power relationship. It also illustrates your ability to laugh at yourself.

For ironic purposes. This sees you showing students that you understand why something really isn't funny (thus making the thing in question funny on a meta-level).

To puncture tension of any form. This sees you using humour to dispel the negative feelings and emotions which can enter the classroom for all manner of different reasons.

Prizes

24 Prizes are essentially contrived goals which you set up in order to motivate your students to do something you want them to do. They are extrinsic motivators (not as powerful as intrinsic ones) which rely on the pupils in question genuinely wanting the prize(s) on offer.

What you offer as a prize is up to you. Don't forget about things such as being the first one to leave the lesson, not having to help tidy up, and winning sought-after responsibilities.

You can offer up prizes to individuals, pairs or teams. You might like to have a number of prizes on offer or just one top prize everyone is attempting to get their hands on.

It is advisable not to overdo the use of prizes. This is because, if prizes become a regular feature of your lessons, students may become less engaged when none are on offer.

Team Games

25 Team games create motivation and engagement because they generate an atmosphere of competition within which students come to identify with their group and therefore want to do well so as to support their teammates (and, possibly, frustrate their competitors).

You can turn most activities into team games by simply asking groups to compete against one another. However, some tasks are much better suited to being team games than others, notably those in which a specific goal is already defined; one which requires input from everyone within a team.

It is important that one judges the use of team games carefully. A balance must be struck between facilitating engagement through competition and ensuring that all members of the class are able to succeed, feel motivated and complete the necessary work.

Meet and Greet

26 Have you ever been into a hotel or department store where somebody is waiting at the door to greet you? The experience is most pleasurable; you feel important; it is as if arrangements have been made in advance, just for you.

The same applies to your classroom.

If you want to motivate and engage your students, stand at your door and welcome them into the lesson. Have the first task already up on the board so that those who pass you can get down to work straight away while you continue to meet and greet pupils who arrive later.

Thank You

27 We just said how nice it is to be welcomed. It is also a really nice feeling when someone thanks you for attending.

Again, we can transfer this fact to the classroom and use it to motivate and engage our pupils.

At the end of your lesson, thank students for their work, their effort and their contributions. Do this to the whole class and then thank pupils individually as they leave. Bid them farewell and point out that you are looking forward to seeing them next lesson. Motivation and engagement are bound to rise as a result.

Karaoke

28 Now this one is a little wacky. But why not?!

Every now and then, introduce a bit of karaoke into your lessons. Take a 2-3 minute break, load up a YouTube karaoke video of a popular song and lead your class in a sing-a-long. This is humorous, fun, out of the ordinary and surprising. Pupils might be dumbfounded at first but they will soon start laughing (and possibly singing). You will foster some positive connotations and break up the lesson in question, raising motivation levels as a result. So go on, give it a try!

Riddles

29 Riddles are great for use at the start of the lesson, regardless of whether or not they connect to the work you will be doing. They quickly engage students (just as they have engaged thousands of readers and listeners since time immemorial), giving them something to think and talk about.

You can find many riddles on the internet – just Google the word 'riddles' and go from there. Here's an old classic to get you started:

What walks on four legs in the morning, two in the afternoon and three at night?

(Answer: Humans. Crawling as a baby; walking as a child and adult; using a stick in old age).

Optical Illusions

30 As with riddles, so too with optical illusions. These are a sure-fire way to generate engagement at the beginning of a lesson. Students can't help but find them interesting; particularly if they are already displayed on the whiteboard as they enter the room.

You can find many optical illusions on the internet. Simply Google 'optical illusions' and away you go!

Movement

31 Sitting at your desk for a long period of time can be quite demotivating. This is partly because the sedentary experience often reinforces itself by luring us into a downward spiral of increasing lethargy.

To combat this, include activities in your lessons which have some movement in them. Here are three easy ones you can use:

When students have completed some individual work, ask them to stand up and share it with three other people.

Present your class with a question and then ask students to find out what three other people think about it who are not sitting near them.

Ask your pupils to stand up and form groups before presenting an activity which these groups need to complete.

Journey into Space

32 You can find many amazing images of space on the internet. Often, these are simply breath-taking.

Engage, motivate and inspire your students by sharing some of these images with them. It doesn't matter if they connect to the lesson or not. The simple fact is that they are amazing!

Here are some sites to have a look at:

http://www.space.com/images/

http://www.spacetelescope.org/images/archive/top 100/

http://www.nasa.gov/multimedia/imagegallery/

The Wonders of the World

33 Not only are the wonders of the universe available to look at online, you can also find the wonders of the world. Again, share these with students whether they connect to your lesson or not. You will inspire them which, in turn, will increase motivation and engagement.

Here are some sites to have a look at:

http://www.nationalgeographic.com/

http://www.britishmuseum.org/

http://www.vam.ac.uk/page/t/the-collections/

http://www.si.edu/

http://www.louvre.fr/en

Pictionary

34 Now we move onto some fun and engaging games you can include as part of your teaching. Once they are in your repertoire, these will always be on hand, ready to use, if a lift in motivation is required.

Pictionary is simple. It works as follows:

Divide the class in half. Write down a list of keywords connected to the topic. Invite a drawer to come to the front from each team in turn. Reveal to them one of the keywords. They then have to draw this on the whiteboard while their team try to guess what the keyword is. No words, letters or numbers are allowed. Nor is the drawer allowed to speak. Teams have 60 seconds to try to guess correctly. The opposing team then have one chance to steal the point if no correct guess has been given.

Play until the list of keywords has been exhausted.

Taboo

35 Taboo is similar to Pictionary except that, instead of drawing the keyword, students have to describe it to their team without using the word itself. They can use any other words they choose but if they say the keyword then they lose the point.

Charades

36 Charades is like Pictionary and Taboo except this time, instead of having to draw the keyword or describe it, students must mime it. They are not allowed to speak although they are free to use gestures and may mime however they wish.

Just a Minute

37 The final of our four games is Just a Minute. This is based on the popular Radio 4 program of the same name. Four students come to the front of the class. The teacher reveals the topic (which connects to the lesson) and the first pupil begins to talk about it.

They are not allowed to repeat anything they say, hesitate or deviate by talking about something off-topic. Their goal is to try to talk about the topic for one minute without repetition, hesitation or deviation.

The class listen and, if they spot any repetition, hesitation or deviation, shout out to indicate the student's error. The topic and the remaining time then passes to the next pupil and the process repeats until the minute is up (the person who is talking when the minute is up is the winner).

Props

38 Create a box of props you can use to liven up your lessons, excite your students, generate engagement and raise motivation.

Props can include:

- Hats

- Equipment connected to your subject

- Items from the past

- Books or magazines

- Accessories

- Disguises

- Random objects

You can use the props yourself or give them out for students to use.

Take on the Role of a Character

39 Instead of being yourself during the lesson, why not take on the role of a character connected to the topic? This doesn't have to be for the whole lesson – it could just be for a short section of it – but it will serve to surprise, engage and motivate your students.

You can use your role-playing as a teaching device by having pupils ask your character questions. Alternatively, you might like to play the game of twenty questions with your class. Here, they have to try to work out who your character is by asking a maximum of twenty questions, all of which must be answerable 'yes' or 'no.'

Give them Independence

40 Moving away from the use of drama, let us now consider some of the broader things you can do while teaching which will encourage motivation and engagement.

First up is giving students independence.

This is something we all want: autonomy and the freedom to make decisions ourselves. In lessons you can facilitate this by:

- Providing pupils with a structure within which to work and express themselves;

- Using activities which are student-led;

- Providing clear success criteria and then leaving it up to students to decide how they achieve these.

Let Students Take Decisions

41 In a similar vein to the previous entry, look to create opportunities for pupils to take decisions. The reasoning behind this is clear. In life, we generally like to feel in control of what we are doing. This fosters a greater engagement with whatever is at issue than the converse.

In addition, if we become habituated into expecting other people to take all our decisions for us, we will most likely end up demotivated and disengaged from the matter in hand. This is because we will see little relevance in it; there will be a disconnect between our own sense of self and the thing in question.

One of the best ways to facilitate student decision-making involves building opportunities for this into the activities you use to deliver your lesson content.

Relevant Connections

42 If you can connect the learning to pupils' lives then you are onto a winner. By making clear the relevance of the lesson content and by showing how this relates to students' day-to-day experiences you will be fostering motivation and giving pupils good reasons to engage with the work.

It is not always possible to make such connections. However, by thinking creatively you should be able to find links more often than not.

Useful Feedback

43 Few students come into lessons actively wanting to do badly. Invariably all pupils want to succeed, although some may find many more barriers to this success than others (and react accordingly).

One of the best ways to help students succeed (and therefore to feel motivated and engaged) is by giving useful feedback – either verbally or in writing.

Useful feedback makes it clear what pupils need to do to improve, how they can make these improvements, and why such improvements will constitute success.

In short, useful feedback is as close to coaching as it is to teaching.

Give Your Class a Theme Tune

44 We now move to a short selection of more unusual ideas which can help to build motivation.

Give your class a theme tune which you play every time they come into your room. This can serve a number of different ends:

- First, if you choose upbeat and energetic music, it will pass on those positive feelings (music is infectious).

- Second, you will begin to condition your students to expect certain things to occur when they hear the music. Therefore, if you are always upbeat, positive and enthusiastic when the music is playing, pupils will come to associate all these traits with the song in question.

- Third, playing a theme tune sends out a message that you are glad to be here, ready to go and ready to have some fun (as well as do some learning); all of which is highly motivational.

Start a Jukebox

45 Here's a great technique to use when students are engaged in a lengthy task.

Hand every pupil in the class a slip of paper. Ask them to write down a song they would like to hear (which is clean and appropriate for playing during a lesson). Collect the song choices in and then start up a jukebox.

Keep the noise to a reasonable volume and make it clear that continued music is dependent on continued work.

The atmosphere in the room will likely lift as a result of this and students will appreciate the sense of give and take (they are giving their hard work and engagement; you are giving a little bit of musical relief).

Roll the Dice

46 Display a slide on your board containing six options. These could be six tasks, six questions, or six possible ways of doing something.

Take a single dice and invite one of your students to roll it. Whatever number comes up, that is the selection (whether it is of a task, question or a way of doing something) the class will pursue.

As you can see, this technique generates excitement and engagement really quickly and easily.

The Fickle Finger of Fate

47 When choosing pupils to answer a question, point a finger towards the class and then begin moving it around at random. Ask a pupil to close their eyes and shout out: 'Stop!'

When they do this, stop your finger.

Whoever the digit is pointing at has to answer the question.

This is The Fickle Finger of Fate. It livens up the most basic of classroom tasks, enthusing pupils at the same time.

Blank Cheque

48 Sometimes, just sometimes, write your students a blank cheque.

Give them a whole lesson, or even just part of a lesson, and ask them to decide what they want to study. Go with their selections. See where it leads you. The results might be surprising or they might not be. Either way, you will have given students independence and the chance to take control.

What is more, the lesson will be remembered by one and all as an unusual change to the routine.

Big Reveal

49 Here's a nice starter activity you can use to build motivation at the beginning of the lesson.

Take an image connected to the topic. Copy and paste it onto a PowerPoint slide. Cover the image with a series of boxes. Use the 'Insert Shapes' function on PowerPoint to do this.

Display the slide to your class and invite pupils to select boxes to remove, one at a time. On each occasion that a box is removed, give students the opportunity to guess what the image beneath is.

Continue until the image is revealed or guessed (the whole process builds tension and excitement as well as encouraging speculation, reasoning and creative thinking).

Give them a Break

50 And so we conclude with one of the best ways to increase motivation and engagement known to humankind. A tried and tested method people have used over thousands of years.

Give students a break.

One minute, two minutes, five minutes. Decide how much time you can spare.

Even a minute can be enough.

A short break will allow pupils to rest their minds before returning re-energised and ready to go.

And don't forget to take a break yourself – you'll need it after using all these ideas to generate huge amounts of engagement and motivation!

A Brief Request

If you have found this book useful I would be delighted if you could leave a review on Amazon to let others know.

If you have any thoughts or comments, or if you have an idea for a new book in the series you would like me to write, please don't hesitate to get in touch at mike@mikegershon.com.

Finally, don't forget that you can download all my teaching and learning resources for **FREE** at www.mikegershon.com.

16735505R00038

Printed in Great Britain
by Amazon